LUKEWARM TEA

LUKEWARM TEA

William Foster

edited by

Tehjae Tsukada

ISBN: 978-1-7779799-0-4

TABLE OF CONTENTS

INTRODUCTION:

LUKEWARM TEA

It was a cup of tea. It wasn't incredible, it wasn't bad. It was exactly as it looked. It was just a lukewarm cup of tea. It was boiled water poured onto leaves, perhaps with added sugar, or honey, or milk, but it was still just a cup of tea. There weren't any embellishments, any tricks, any hidden features, or new ideas. There was just boiled water and tea leaves. The tea was forgotten, neglected, and ignored so it turned lukewarm.

The tea wasn't new. There weren't any surprises about the cup of tea. The tea was common, a manufactured product that we were accustomed to, an essential part of our lives, alongside coffee and water. We've all seen an abandoned, irrelevant, unimportant cup of tea sitting on a counter, slowly going cold. We ignored that cup of tea because we didn't care about that cup of tea. We didn't even realize our apathy towards that cup of tea because we put no conscious thought into the cup of tea or our reaction to it, slowly cooling, sitting there.

It was a cup of tea.

It was not evil. It was not good.

It wasn't holding anything you wouldn't expect from a cup of tea.

It was there, resting on that counter, left for a bit too long, but still somewhat warm, still somewhat palatable.

It was yet another cup of lukewarm tea.

MY FAMILY

My Ma, my mother's mom, once told me how she stared down the blade of a machete. She haltingly told me how she was robbed, how her gold, silver, jewelry, and money were stolen from her. She told me about the pirates that attacked her family just off the coast of southern Vietnam. She described her pain and worry as she prepared for the boat trip, how she gave her three daughters, aged eight months, three years, and five years old, as many valuables as they could hold. She told me how she hid jewelry and gold bars amongst their clothing. She described her despair while explaining to her five-year-old daughter that they were going to get robbed while she filled her daughters clothing with jewelry and money. My Ma told me how difficult it was to stuff her infant daughter's clothing with cold, heavy silver and gold, but she did it anyway. She knew the pirates and robbers wouldn't search an infant's clothes.

She described her pain when she watched men she'd known her entire life, men she'd known since their childhood, men she'd helped to raise and nurture like one of her own children, rob her loved ones at machete point. She described the guilt in their faces, the poverty in their clothes and the hunger in their emaciated bodies. She described her hopelessness as she lost her livelihood for the second time, now by her old friends' hands.

She told me those men, those pirates, those robbers, those thieves, those bandits, pointed her in the right direction to get out of South Vietnam, told her where the communist military was patrolling, told her which countries were accepting Vietnamese refugees. She told me how they helped her escape the communists, because they'd known her and her family and her friends their whole life and wished they could help her instead of robbing her.

She described her frustration, her helplessness, when she was forcibly removed from her home in South Vietnam by the communists, when they took away her house, her business, her life— her future. She told me how she and my Goung, my mother's dad, my Ma's husband, refused to suffer and rot and toil as slaves over a miserable swamp in the middle of nowhere. She told me how she refused to live in exile in her own country.

This was one of my few memories with Ma, and among the earliest. She wasn't fluent in English. I didn't learn Mandarin or Cantonese or Vietnamese. I needed an aunt, or an uncle, or some other relative to translate Ma's words. I didn't speak with her much. I didn't ask about where she came from, what her family history was, until later in my childhood. My strongest memory of her was food: the incredible, delicious, wonderous amounts of food that she and her husband made and bought every week when we went to her house.

Throughout my childhood, I consumed digital media: E-books, movies, television, video games, the internet. They dominated my life. I never considered how I received these entertainments, nor the struggle my family endured to bring these entertainments into my life. I didn't want for anything. I took these luxuries for granted. I never tried to learn the full story of what my family went through to get me where I am today. I never asked. I only learned pieces of a larger narrative.

I discovered excerpts, snippets of an incomplete story, my family's story, my story.

My grandfather, on my dad's side, didn't talk much about his past, and he wasn't enthusiastic when I asked him about it. He loved talking about his life in Canada, about his sons, his house projects, his jobs, his wife, but when I asked him about Scotland, he paused. He gave serious thought to his words. When Scotland came up, he carefully selected what we talked about and chose which questions he wanted to answer. He guided our talks, ensured we only discussed his topics. He was a large man, tattooed, muscled and brutally honest. He spoke his mind. He had no qualms about cursing or swearing or offending.

My brother and I used to follow him around, no matter where he went, even when he didn't want us to. When he'd leave to smoke on the balcony, we'd sneak out and follow him outside, even while he tried to keep away from us, telling us to stay away from his cigarette smoke. We never listened to him though, because "We want to see you Grandad!". He loved to tell that story.

I think grandad wished he'd forgotten Glasgow. He said that Glasgow was different then, at least where he lived. He wasn't specific. Grandad described unemployment, gangs, drugs, violence, and death. He told me about people you shouldn't, couldn't, wouldn't, cross. He told me about the people who were never seen again, who vanished from society. He told me about the families that never learned what happened to their loved ones, the friends and lovers who stopped crying years ago, the loved ones who had long since given up hope. He told me about the economic troubles of the 1970's for the people of Glasgow, but he wasn't specific.

He told me how he was one of the people who wasn't crossed in Glasgow,

He told me his favorite weapon was a can opener—

The old kind, like a cross between a set of pliers and a wrench.

He told me the can opener was his favorite weapon because it never, ever, left a clean wound. He said it mangled and severed its way through flesh and bone alike.

He told me that can openers always left a scar, a permanent reminder of the mistake, the failure, that person made, a constant reminder of why they should've respected my grandad.

He told me how people never disrespected him twice.

He told me how people never forgot how badly they lost.

He didn't tell me whether he didn't give anyone a second chance to respect him.

In 1975, the Vietnam War was lost to the communists. My mother's family, owners of a successful business in South Vietnam, refused the swamps, the pitiful farmland, they were forcibly moved to, and fled Vietnam by boat. After great difficulty, they made their way to Canada.

My father's family left Scotland by plane, arriving in Canada, when my dad was two years old. My grandad was a successful man, you could say.

My father has no memories of a childhood in Scotland, nor does my mother in Vietnam. My Mom was five when her family, when she, arrived in Canada.

One of mother's earliest memories was an elementary school party. They had chocolates and candy and cupcakes and ice cream. When the food was served, she asked someone next to her if she could eat their salad, which was the appetizer. Mom had never seen nor eaten salad before, and she loved it and wanted more. Mom never forgot the look on her teacher's face when she asked for more salad over chocolate, because, as she said, "salad was more interesting".

I was born in Brampton, and my family moved to Mississauga not long afterward. My story started with my family: me, my mother, my father, and my brother.

My story started with a woman who was sitting at her mother in law's dining table. She was wracked with stress and worry. She held an infant in her arms and a little boy played by her feet. She was trying to figure out how she and her husband, at 22 years old, were going to support two little boys, let alone themselves. She was splitting her attention between the economics textbook, the notes she'd written, the bills and loans spread across the table, and her two young children.

My family's story was one of perseverance, a story of skill and sheer force of will. My father left his dead-end retail job for a position at *Canada Post* and then my mother received her education at the *University of Toronto Mississauga*. She got a job working at a bank, and later, landed a job at the *U of T Mississauga Library*. She finally paid her student loans 30 years later.

My earliest memory of mom was when I dumped several crayons into the heating vent. I was three. I watched her scrub the wall and the heater clean of plastic muck from the corner of our residence on the *U of T Mississauga* campus. Mom was going through her economics degree, before she started working, before she landed her job at the *U of T Mississauga Library*.

Another early memory was of elementary school, when my friend introduced my family to their family after class. We were constantly together after that meeting, our families visited each other daily. We formed a tightly knit unit that lasted until middle school. At our peak, my friend spent more time at my house than he did his own.

Throughout my life, I was fascinated by the internet and video games. I spent tens of thousands of hours glued to a computer, a television, or a console. I played games with my friends, not realizing the incredible ethnic diversity amongst us: From Somalia to India to China to Japan to The United Kingdom, to Poland, I was, unwittingly, a part of the multicultural experiment of Mississauga and the Greater Toronto Area.

In high school, my friend group drifted away from one another, as friend groups sometimes did in high school. We were starting to notice the happenings of the world. The world was changing, just exiting the recession of 2008, and I needed to figure out what I'd do with the rest of my life. My friends all wanted to go far in life, to create a better world, to find wealth and prosperity and success, to find love and happiness, to travel to unique places across Western Europe, The United States, Japan, South Korea, Australia, and so on.

I didn't have those great ambitions.

Eventually, I graduated high school, and applied to the *University of Toronto Mississauga*. As I entered *UTM* for the first time, before my first semester started, I was walking with my mother and brother. We'd received the letter that both my brother and I were accepted into *U of T Mississauga*. We'd followed mom to work so we could learn the campus' layout and have some idea where to go when we arrived for class.

As we walked towards the library, we came across a doe munching on leaves. It was the first time I paid attention to the environment around me, beyond the pathways and structures that led me to my next destination. I watched the doe as it meandered about the campus, munching on vegetation, ignoring the people there, apathetic to my presence, apathetic to humans, apathetic to the university. It was the same year that Ma died, less than a year after Goung died, the same year I realized I'd never get my family's full story.

Watching that doe as it munched on leaves, I felt neutral to that doe. I observed its calm walk through the campus. I didn't watch it for long. Watching that doe, I realized my love of observing and absorbing the world around me. I realized that I enjoyed watching the world pass by me, reveling in the apathy and wonder of the world around me. I realized how little I knew of the world, how fractured my understanding of the world was. I realized I wanted to learn by walking through the world, learn by watching the smallest creatures and the largest skyscrapers, learn from the greatest of people and the most inconsequential of animals. I wanted to see these people and places live, go about their lives, find joy in their lives, find love in their lives, live their lives.

I realized how unprepared I was for the world ahead of me.

I realized that I couldn't understand what Ma told me. I couldn't comprehend the experience of staring death in the eye, watching as your whole life collapsed before you, watching as people tore your livelihood away from you. I wouldn't learn what Glasgow was once like, I wouldn't have a favorite weapon, nor would I see what made my grandad hesitate when I asked him about his youth, about Scotland, about Glasgow. As that doe wandered away, I hoped those facts remained true. I hoped, instead, I'd experience the world of the Greater Toronto Area: I would experience the world my family brought me to, I would try to understand what their experiences meant and where my story would take me. I would live the life they provided me and learn from what I pieced together about my past.

I would try to not squander their efforts.

I wouldn't squander their efforts.

SIX YEARS

"Hey William! It's great to see you here!" a voice called from behind me.

It was Jason.

"Hi." I mustered a small smile.

"Hi Jessica, Dylon, Ben!" he nodded to my family.

"My condolenc- "

"Thank you. I wasn't very close to Great Grandpa, so I'm more here for my dad than me! I'll pass your condolences to him. He'll appreciate them."

Jason was always chipper, always had a smile on his face. He looked at the positive side of every situation. He found ways to make people happy with themselves, with their lives. He made you happy through his confidence, by embracing who he was, by embracing who you were, by making you feel better about everything and anything with his assuredness and stability. Jason was a smart guy, likable, handsome, tall, well spoken, charismatic, popular, easygoing—

The opposite of me.

"Anyways, thanks for coming to the funeral! Even though it's here, I'm really glad to see you again! How's your life been Will?"

Jason was comfortable to talk to. He had a natural magnetism, a personality that others couldn't match, an honesty that relaxed people, that made conversation and friendship with him easy. They made any relationship with him relaxed and comfortable. From his girlfriend to his best friends to his acquaintances to people I was sure he didn't like, they all enjoyed talking to him. People were with him because they wanted his company and he welcomed them with open arms.

"About the same, nothing really different. It's been okay."

I lied so easily it was impressive. When I was confronted with honesty, I hid behind a veil of formality, of norms, of conventions, of dishonesty. When I was shown real interest in my life, when I was shown compassion, kindness, and good-natured acceptance of my person, of my character, of me, I callously turned my back and ran away. I shunned my friend's empathy, my family's love, my colleagues' approval, my peer's comradery. I hid from their love, I fled from their friendship. I refused what they freely gave.

I ran away, cowardly, and foolishly.

Jason grinned. "That's good! I've been playing *Civilization V*! Have you ever played it?"

I smiled. My eyes were blank, empty, and hollow. My face was devoid of emotions or color, greyed, unfeeling, and generic. "Yeah, I've played it".

Video games were one of his default conversations with me.

Jason could talk to anyone and make them like him, no matter who they were, what they liked, or where they met. From *Erindale Secondary* to *Square One*, from *Gucci* and *Rolex* to *Super Mario Bros* and *The Avengers*, from *Pride and Prejudice* to Golf, he pulled conversation with others from nowhere. He found exactly what interested them and was enthused by their excitement, their passion, their love for it. He didn't ignore your words, he listened. He gave you his full attention, he internalized every word you said, and he responded, actively and passionately, in kind. His own familiarity with the subject was irrelevant because you felt comfortable talking to him. People liked talking to Jason.

He made you feel important.

"What about the fourth *Civilization* game? I've really been liking that one. It just works better for me! You know my laptop, hey! The thing could barely run *Minecraft*!"

I met Jason in senior kindergarten. *Sawmill Valley Public School* and *Erindale Secondary* provided me so many friendships that I methodically tore apart, so many people, so many friends, so many peers, that couldn't look me in the eye anymore, people that I couldn't look in the eye anymore, people that I was ashamed to look in the eye anymore.

I cut our friendship apart. I severed my friendships one by one, shredded each relationship I'd formed. I ran from them, fled into myself, fled towards isolation, emptiness, nothingness. I fled because I couldn't accept my failures. I couldn't accept my emotions, my love, my face, my body, my desires, my hope, my anger, my hatred.

I couldn't look at myself in the mirror.

I hated what I saw in the mirror.

Jason was my closest friend in elementary school. We spent every moment together. He came over to my house every day, every weekend, every week, every month, every year.

"No, I played Civ Revolution though." My face trembled, my mouth twitched and spasmed, my throat locked up. My mom looked at me. I refused to meet her gaze.

Jason smiled "Oh yeah, that one was good too. Well, it was great to see you again! I'm gonna go talk to my parents and sister. Okay?"

My smile shook, my eyes twitched. Mom looked back to Jason.

"Yeah. Bye. Tell Maria, Moe and Sarah I said hi." I grimaced.

I barely saw him in *Erindale Secondary*. I didn't speak with him much.

No.

He spoke to me.

I didn't listen to him.

Jason nodded as he turned away. "I'll see you on the web." His finger guns were somehow natural, not uncomfortable, not awkward, not depressing, not sad.

I haven't seen Jason in six years.

THE IPAD

I bit into my BLT sandwich. Oil and grease oozed onto my hands. "Uncle Albert said he'd give us $50? That means we have just enough to buy it then, right?"

Ben nodded.

Mom chewed through her own bite "Yeah, everyone's pitched in. He said he'd give us the money after we bought it, so we can go whenever—" she abruptly took another bite.

We looked towards Dad as he slid the backdoor open.

"Dad, what did you mean when you said, "you attract weirdos?"" Ben asked.

Dad marched across the kitchen, planting one hand on the countertop. "Okay, so I was walking out of the plant towards the car, I was at about the middle of the parking lot. I'd just carded out of work and was passing the loading docks and the delivery trucks. I was answering one of my employees' questions about the protocols for the sorting belts, it was something about safety procedures and gloves—"

I quirked an eyebrow "Wow, gloves? That does sound like a weirdo. Does he always ask questions, the prick? I bet he loves doing that! Talking to people, asking question, socializing with his boss and co-workers, Goddamn, why's everyone such a weirdo these days!?!?" I chomped my BLT. "Can't have a civilized conversation with anyone!" I giggled through my mouthful.

Dad sighed.

I choked on my BLT.

"Anyways, this guy is in socks and sandals, a *Canada's Wonderland* T-shirt, and blue cargo shorts, walked up to me. Remember, I'm in my full *Canada Post* uniform, in a *Canada Post* parking lot, and it's 3:30pm, around when shifts change, so there were plenty of people leaving the post office, all in their *Canada Post* uniforms."

"You good?" Ben quirked an eyebrow at me.

I gasped for breath. "Yeah —*cough— yeah, I'm fine."

Dad looked at the clock. "I need to flip the steak, gimme a sec."

We watched dad walk out the door. It slid closed behind him with a clack.

*Cough

Mom looked at Ben. "We're going to the mall tomorrow, so uh, we can go to the Apple store then and I'll make something up. I'll go with the Granddad idea." She turned to me "Which *iPad* model did you say we were buying?"

"Uh, the 5th generation *iPad*. The $329 one."

"Okay" Mom pointed at me. "You can't spill the beans!"

I scoffed. "Mom, we're equally terrible at acting. I'm more surprised he hasn't figured it out yet. We weren't exactly subtle when we asked everyone else to pitch in!" I patted myself on the back. "Good job William! Good—"

The sliding glass door slid open.

"So, I saw this guy just as he saw me, and the dude started running over. So, I said "Hello, may I help you?" I figured he really wanted to ask me a question, maybe he'd ordered a parcel or mail, or maybe he knew someone in the plant, or maybe he knew the guy I was talking to, or maybe SOMETHING to do with *Canada Post*, the place I obviously worked at and was walking out of!" Dad sat at the table, fiddling with his timer.

"He stopped about 50 feet away, looked me right in the eye, dusted himself off, and strutted over. The way he walked, jeez, you'd swear he owned the entire post office or something. He flipped his head back and screamed at me, "You know, I got superpowers! I'm a clairvoyant! Right!"."

We stared at Dad.

My right ear almost touched to my right shoulder. "Okay?" I asked.

Mom and Ben nodded in confusion. "What?"

Dad laughed "Right?! I just nodded and said to the guy "Uh huh." and the guy started nodding too, like I'd proved his genius or something like that. He started waving his arms at me, yelling "So, that means I can see the future! I'm a clairvoyant, you know! They never believed me, but I showed them!! I got superpowers!!!" He started pacing in circles, throwing his hands around like he was making a presidential speech or something."

Dad laughed. "The guy looked at the sky with this weird expression on his face and said "So, I thought to myself, I think *Canada Post* is gonna be a good deal! I know it'll be a good deal! The future is telling me *Canada Post* will be a damn good deal! So, if you can buy *Canada Post* Stocks you should do it!" He started pointing at me, triumphantly, arrogantly staring down his nose at me."

Mom furrowed her eyebrows "Wait, you can buy *Canada Post* stocks—"

"Nope. It's a crown corporation" Ben chortled.

I laughed "Oh God, I see what you mean." I put on a terrible American accent. "And one day, I'm gonna find that kitty, get my wife back, get my kids, get that house, build that spaceship, and fly to the MOON!!!"

Dad sighed. "Yeah. I just nodded to him, and he kept yelling at me to buy *Canada Post* stocks, "since I'm always right about the future! I'm a clairvoyant! I've never been wrong!"" Dad chuckled. "He started yelling that at the other workers, going on and on and on about "*Canada Post* Stocks" and "the future" and his "secret powers" and the "secret government agents", and then he just left."

Dad slumped over the table. "He just walked away, humming a stupid song, like he'd never said a thing!" Dad threw his arms up in the air.

Dad sighed. "Why do I attract idiots?"

Dad's timer began beeping. He stood up from the table.

We were quiet for a moment. Dad strode out the backdoor.

We all looked out the window. Rain started to pour onto my dad's umbrella. The water sizzled as it reached the open barbeque. The aluminum foil covered my dad's steak. It plinked and crinkled with freshwater droplets.

"Wet socks in sandals!" Mom shuddered.

I nodded. "Ugh."

Ben chuckled. "Jeez."

I looked at mom and Ben. "So, we'll buy it tomorrow."

"Yep."

"Okay."

I covered my face with my hand. "Dammit." I grinned like a fool.

Mom glared at me with a small smirk locked on her face. "Shhh!"

"What?" Dad squinted at us. We passed *Forever 21* and *LensCrafters* as we walked to the *Apple* store. He stared Mom down. "What did I say?"

"Nothing" Ben shook his head. "By the way, William, have you seen the new *Call of Duty* trailer? What do you think about how it's set in World War 2—
"

"What did I say? Why're you smiling?" Dad interrupted.

We quietly walked past *Second Cup*.

"I asked if "anyone knew where the *Apple* store was so we could buy your Grandad's new *iPad*, the *iPad* you wanted to buy for his birthday?" And then you started giggling?" Dad looked from Mom to me. "That's the reason we came to *Square One*. What's so funny about that?"

"Ugh. This is why you two shouldn't play poker." Ben sighed.

"Shhh!!" Mom placed a finger against her lips.

Dad narrowed his eyes at Ben and Mom. He whipped his head towards me. He stepped closer, entering my space. His green eyes stared me down, stared into my mind, stared into my very soul.

You know, *Kernel's Popcorn* smelled so good. Man, I loved popcorn—

Dad stepped in front of me "William"—

Usually, I thought it was gross, and that popcorn stuck to my teeth, but I really wanted some *caramel Kernel's Popcorn* or even *Double Hit Kernel's Popcorn.* Oh, just thinking about it made my mouth water. It'd taste so good! I feel nauseous already! —

Dad poked me in the shoulder "William, look at me"—

Maybe I should buy some— *Poke

"William"—

After all, we've walked this entire time, and we all could use a break, a cheat day, and it tastes so good, even with the teeth thing—

"William, stop ignoring me."—

Just imagine, the salty buttery flavour, the sickly-sweet caramel, the decadent, luscious, diabetes-inducing sugar coated—

Dad poked me again. "William. Why are we here? What did you do? What's going on?"—

Though, popcorn was always mom's favorite, so I should ask if she wants some—

"William "—

I leaned around Dad's head "Mom do you want some *Kernel's* popcorn?"

She snorted. "No thanks."

"Okay." I chirped.

Dad stopped. His brow furrowed. "We're not buying this *iPad* for your Grandad, are we?"

I tripped over my own foot.

Dad grabbed my arm, yanking me back on balance, hoisting me to his side. "Who are we buying this *iPad* for?"

I looked to Ben and Mom. Ben shook his head, sighing, both hands plastered on his face. Mom shrugged. Her cheeks blossomed into a full smile. Giggles leaked out from behind her hands. I opened my mouth, but no words came out.

Dad moved in front of me again. "Who are we buying this iPad for?"

I stared at him. "Grandad?"

"Was that a question? Are you asking me? Because this was your idea, right? To buy Grandad an *iPad* for his birthday, which, coincidently, is just weeks after my birthday?" Dad grinned at me.

I stared at him. My mouth flopped around like a goldfish out of its fishbowl.

"You wanted to buy Grandad a new *iPad*, which is why you've asked me so many times about my old *iPad 2*? The *iPad* I kept telling you I wanted to replace???" Dad's smile stretched across his whole face.

I kept my mouth shut.

He let go of me with a grin.

We walked silently to the *Apple* store. We entered the *Apple* store.

Dad stroked his beard, humming along the aisle. "Hmmm. Should we get Grandad a 32 GB *iPad* or a 128 GB *iPad*? Hmmm."

"32GB"

"Pardon me?" Dad smirked at me.

"I- we- we're buying Grandad a 32GB 5th generation *iPad*." I sulked.

Dad smiled "Ah, I see." He took Grandad's new *iPad* to the counter.

I muttered to myself. "Yeah. We uh, we were buying Grandad a new *iPad*, definitely, absolutely."

I stood in line with my family. Dad happily thumbed Grandad's new *iPad*. "Thanks, you guys!" he smiled

I sighed.

"Ben."

"Yes William."

"You were right."

"I was."

I handed him a loonie. I looked at my feet.

"I'm never playing poker."

"No, you shouldn't."

I walked into the living room and slumped onto the couch.

"William! Thanks again for getting everyone to buy me a new iPad! It's great! I love it!" Dad hugged me.

I sighed. "You're welcome, Dad." I hugged him back.

UNFORTUNATE TIMING

"I'll go do the book drop."

"'kay"

I walked towards the front of the library as my cart squeaked along the neat, grey tiles, my hand clutched the book drop keys. I approached the book drop with almost indecent haste. I franticly opened the doors and placed the books and Ziploc bags on my book cart.

I glanced over my shoulder.

Becky was clicking away at a computer. Jamie was flipping through a large binder.

I walked the cart back towards the Information and Loans (ILS) desk. I kept my eyes firmly on my book cart.

"Jamie, I'll take my Break around 12:30" Becky said without looking away from her computer.

"Okay" she replied, rifling through her own book cart, one hand holding a specific page in her binder open.

I grimaced to myself, though I managed to turn it into a small nod. I rolled past my co-workers with abated breath. I watched the wheels roll over the worn carpet, roll over the patterns and breaks in the carpet's design. My cart rolled along the ILS desk, then the shelves, then the computer. I turned towards the processing computer behind the ILS desk. I stopped.

I stared at the barren desk, the barren sorting carts, the empty workspace. I stared at the books, the manuals, the journals, the inanimate objects that rested on the desk.

I breathed. I exhaled.

I relaxed.

I started scanning the book drop materials into the *SirsiDynix* computer system.

I pushed my book cart out of the elevator and walked towards the stacks. The full book cart teetered along the grey carpet, its wheels squeaking along the pathway as I adjusted the collar of my uniform and moved the cart towards the A-K bookshelves. The cart's old dirty wheels screeched under the weight of dozens of books, piercing through the quiet rows of bookshelves. I walked past the group study area, away from the rustle of paper and pens, the clicking and clacking of laptop keyboards, the hiss of coats and sweaters and stage-whispered conversation. I passed the A-K sign. I entered the A shelves and picked up the first book on my book cart. I began shelving my books, slowly making my way through the shelves. My cart slowly emptied. Its wheels stopped squeaking. The old wheels were finally able to handle the load.

I paused. I craned my head out of the C shelves, gazing at the E and F shelves.

Surely, I heard that wrong, right? A soft moan, low, almost pained, whispered across the third floor of the *University of Toronto Mississauga Library*. A grunt, A low, hushed, monotone groan that contrasted the orderly, silent library floor.

I turned back to my shelving, but my hand froze halfway to my book cart. There the noise was again. I stepped out of the C shelves.

"Hello?" I winced, my voice screamed back at me, scratchy, rough, and abrasive. Its cadence blasted my ears and reverberated down the stacks. Silence returned to the library.

I watched my book cart, ears perked. No sounds followed. I leaned against the shelf, listening. I heard the whir of the air conditioning units. I heard the distant clip of high heels on stairs. I heard the hum of computer fans and the rustling of clothing and the scritch of pencils on paper and the clack of laptop keyboards. I heard small snippets of distant conversation and the crinkle of books and paper.

I grasped a book from the end my book cart and looked at its call number. It's an F shelf book. I abandoned my cart and skulked toward the F shelves. I clawed the F shelf book in my trembling hand. I pressed the book into my chest, a barrier for my racing heart, a shield against the unknown. A gentle voice, muffled, restrained, muted, quiet, halting, hesitant, eager, murmured into the stacks. The voice was getting louder, less restrained. I approached D. I passed D. I approached E. I passed E. I approached F.

"Hi, may I help you---"

I whipped back around "SORRY!"

"Oh shi---!"

"Wha---?!?"

"Fu---!!!"

I marched back to my book cart in the C shelves, frantic zippers, clothing, and expletives ringing out behind me.

I stared at the C shelves. I stared at the remaining books on my book cart. One minute passed.

I re-adjusted my collar.

I didn't watch a man and woman leave the F shelves.

I didn't see their blushing faces, nor their abashed expressions.

I did not see them leave the library.

I did not see anything because I stared resolutely at my book cart and waited.

I walked my cart back to the sorting area.

I stared at my half empty cart.

I stared at the other book carts filled with books.

I decided to shelve L to Z instead.

SWEET DREAMS

Ben sat at his computer. The clouded night sky was hidden by his dark curtains. The battle was coming. Steel armor plates glinted in the morning sunlight as the tanks moved into position. The caster's frantic voice boomed alongside the first volley of canon fire. The tanks deafening guns cracked into the first wave of hostile infantry and armor. At the tanks side, friendly infantry zipped to and from defensive positions, their metal rifles clattering against their armor, their bullets rattling into the valley. The first line held against the onslaught of hostile forces and started a slow retreat to the second defensive line. The assault was renewed by the second wave of infantry and armor, as they threw themselves into the defensive line. Reinforcements streamed into the fight, supplementing the remaining infantry, and destroyed vehicles. Bang! Thump! Bang! Thump! The hostile infantry swarmed past the cement bunkers and auto turrets, as the enemy armor obliterated their ranks with concentrated fire and volleys. The hostiles approached the main entrance. The hostile armor punctured the walls and defensive systems with their guns, brutally sweeping through the workers frantically repairing the faltering line. Each unit of the defensive line was subjected to a constant barrage of machine gun and artillery fire. Jet fighters screamed overhead, their gargantuan machine gun rounds and missiles colliding with one another. Bang! Thump! Bang! Thump! The challenger's forces were going to win— wait, what?

Ben lowered his computer's volume. Was that the stream or a door closing just outside his bedroom? He paused for a moment, raising a headphone off his head, listening. The house was quiet. Wind audibly blew through the old house. The Canadian winter howled on. Was there something that Ben forgot about? No, there was no way! It was almost 1:00AM! Mom and Dad usually fell asleep before 9:00PM, let alone 1:00AM! There was no way anyone else was awake— Oh, damn, it was 1:00AM. The soft noise of the stream was all Ben heard. He sat and waited. Thump!

Ben took his headphones off. There it was again. He waited. He was the only one awake. He heard nothing. Ben's door frame was darkly lit by his ceiling light, its white shape not quite visible in the dimly lit room. It was quiet. Ben shrugged, placing his headphones back over ears, and returned to the *StarCraft* stream. Maybe it finally happened, and Dad wasn't kidding when he said the Fosters all lose their minds eventually. Regardless, it probably wasn't important. If it was, William or Mom would text him about it in the morning, assuming something had happened at all.

The clock read 2:30AM. Whoops. Switching the PC off, Ben stood. His tired, bleary eyes blinked into the dark hallway. There was little sound, the silence only broken by intermittent shivering and soft exhales. The hallway was dimly lit by Ben's ceiling light. Down the hall, there was blackness. The bathroom door was slightly ajar, and the master bedroom's double doors were closed. Down the other way, William's door was closed. Finally, just outside Ben's room, there he was. Normally, Ben didn't care if William stood around his bedroom door, but the specific way that William leaned against the wall, his eyes closed, his head slack against his left shoulder, his shoulders slumped forwards, his half naked body shivering and shuddering in the cool dark hallway, was slightly concerning. If William wanted to stand around half naked, leaning against the wall, right outside his bedroom door in the middle of the night, that was his right, but Ben wasn't sure this was a conscious decision. Shivering again, William's face was calm, expressionless even. His eyes were a flurry of motion behind his eyelids. His teeth gently chattered. He, drunkenly, slowly, slovenly, slid down the wall, hunched over with his head almost level with his shoulders. Ben gave a deep sigh, "William? What are you doing?"

William didn't respond. His face slowly drooped further down. His glasses were pushed to the side of his face, sticking out perpendicular to his cheek. He leaned heavier against the wall. Drool seeped onto his chest.

"Heh. Heh. Heh." Ben tried to suppress his chuckles.

Ben leaned down, inspecting William's trembling form. "Uhm," was as far as Ben got, when William's mouth opened.

"No. No. No. Nnnnn I Can't. It's— hem. The uhh, I would but mm. Um. Uh? No? Pu-reh. I really wan— hmm uh hrn." William pushed off the wall and then collapsed back against it. Thump!

Ben slowly smiled as he listened to his brother's inane rambling. William's mouth lulled open again as words tumbled out in a frantic gibbering rush.

"Hum, Ha, Pre, Tee, Pro, Pot, Eh, At, how abou— Do, Do, Do you want, Dooooo"

Thump!

Chuckling, Ben opened William's bedroom door. William's blankets and covers were folded up towards the foot of the bed. Sometimes, it's easy to forget what your family used to do, until it happens again. William hadn't sleepwalked for years. Regardless, that wasn't important, William needed to go back to bed. Trying to avoid the drool spread across his brother's torso, Ben pressed his hand onto William's shoulders. Ben slowly walked back towards William's bedroom, holding an unresisting brother under his shoulder. "Okay, let's get you back to bed?" Ben's muffled laughs concealed some of his words. He led his sleeping brother into the room, moving through the doorway.

"No n- it wa- was— bad— hm. Hnnn. Nooooo, mmmmhhh. It wu-hnn-guh. Garbage, Gar, garr, Garn, marn, Har".

Ben chuckled "Alright William get back in— yeah? Uh. Yes. Yup exactly?" With a bemused expression, he watched his brother lift his bed's blankets, slip off his glasses, place his glasses on his night table, lie down under the blankets, and pull them back over his body. The winter wind blew through the dark house. Ben watched his sleeping brother, cheerily snoozing away like he wasn't just standing upright, half naked, outside his brother's room at 2:30AM. Ben closed the bedroom door behind him.

"God Damn William." He laughed.

Honestly, William was lucky. Normally, Ben and dad wouldn't give William so much time to stew in his own embarrassment, as he waited with abated breath for them to pounce on him. They almost never gave him four whole weeks of not hearing the same jokes and same stories from a decade ago, especially when he sleepwalked. Father and brother insisted every time that they weren't lying, that William did sleepwalk. William had no memories of sleep walking. He didn't know how or why or when or where he did it, but his family swore that they saw him sleep walking constantly when he was a kid.

Mother and father laughed even harder at Ben's story.

Honestly, William didn't remember what the original stories were, especially about his sleepwalking. No one was interested in telling the actual version. Even when the original was mentioned, they silently agreed to tell the exaggerated stories instead. Whether the story's authentic accurate version was a great story, even when everyone, including William, agreed that the original story was the actual story, the family went with the ridiculous version anyway. Eventually, everyone forgot the original vs the actual version because no one cared to remember the difference. The stories were more exaggerated, more ridiculous, more absurd, and more outlandish, every time they told the story, but William didn't mind. After all, what storyteller didn't add a little flair, a little extra, a little more drama, to their favorite stories. His family loved a good story, and these were among their favorites. William took their word that the stories were true, or at least were true at one point. Granted, he took their word with a grain, or large pile, of salt.

"Here we go again" William smirked as mom and dad started going on and on about another sleepwalking story.

The day was uneventful. Night had come and everyone was asleep. Even the resident night owl, Ben, was snoring away in his bed. Around 2 AM, an event started to happen, an event which no one predicted. The family would remember what happened on that fateful day. Regardless of the inexorable march of time, regardless of a person's wish to forget, the family remembered the events that occurred during the waning hours of an uneventful night.

William staggered into the hallway. His head lolled to the side. His eyes were closed. In the darkness, only the shadow of his body was visible, framed against the clear moon lit sky. His blank, unseeing stare locked on the double doors opposite his room. His body reflected on the hallway mirror. He stumbled, fell, shuffled, and slithered across the hallway, haltingly, slowly, moaning his way towards the door.

"Gym. Jim. Gym. Jim." His voice murmured into the hallway. His breaths echoed inside the cramped space. He gradually, eventually, arrived at the double door. "Gym. Gym. Jimmm". His shuffling was barely audible in the dark, quiet hallway. The door opened with little fanfare: The creak of an old door, the slap of flesh on metal, the groans of a little boy, the trembles of small feet on carpet, these sounds wafted into the now open master bedroom. The boy paused. His head turned, unseeing, unflinching, and expressionless, towards his parent's bed. Father's snoring was audible, but not overwhelmingly so. The mounds of mom and dad rose and fell with their measured breaths. The calming, deafening, ringing, constant cacophony of their breathing filled the quiet room.

"Gym. Jim. Gym. Jim." Was whispered throughout the bedroom.

The foot of the bed was made of wood, its polished texture was soft on the boy's hand. The bedsheets whispered against the boy's skin, tightly squeezed between his small fingers. The blankets and sheets whipped through the air, landing on Dad's sleeping body. Dad's knees, dad's feet, dad's ankles were exposed to the air, to the hand smoothing out the wrinkled bed sheets covering dad's body. The texture was smooth, soft, against the boy's hand, warm against his skin, warmed by his father's body, warmed by his father's legs, warmed by his father's feet, warmed by his father's ankle. The trembling hand reached out to dad's ankle. The murmuring increased in volume, getting louder, faster, angrier, more desperate, more frantic, more aggressive.

"Gymm. Jimm. Gym! Jimm! Gym. Jimmmm!! Gymmm!! Gymmmm!!! Jimmmmm!!!!!"

He clenched his fist around the ankle and began to squeeze. His chanting rose, the hand clasped as tightly as it could against the soft skin and hard bone under it. The leg kicked reflexively, but his grip held firm, clamping onto the vulnerable, exposed, bruised, pale ankle.

"Wha-? Uh-" "Huh?" Dad jolted awake, waking mom in the process. They lifted their heads to the foot of their bed. The boy was there, screeching at the ankle. His face was obscured by his hair, his shoulders were wracked with pains. His hand was throbbing and shuddering and trembling and spasming with pressure.

"William?" Mom whispered. Jostled by the spasming leg he was clenching, the boy's grasp tightened with every movement. His arm visibly shook from the pressure of clenching his fist so hard. His muttered whispers turned into screams, a fevered pitch reverberating in the room, the boy's head, the boy's entire body, started to fold in on itself, the ankle lifting from the mattress as he screamed at it right in his face.

"Gym! Jim! Gym! Jim! Gym! Jim! Gy—"

The boy abruptly halted. William's head turned without his body to his parents. Sweat dribbled down his forehead, his eyes a fury of motion behind his closed eyelids. His hand started to release its staunch grip on dad's ankle. He began to breathe, gasp, wheeze, heavy and audible, "They're coming They're coming They're coming They're coming". His Father's leg, almost free, was grabbed by both hands. The boy's hair whipped against his face as he stared at the damnable ankle. The boy squeezed his grip as tightly as he could. His words boomed across the darkened room.

With an audible gulp and a wince of pain, Dad's mouth trembled open. "Who is coming?" Dad whimpered. His voice was almost inaudible against the boy's zealous chanting.

The boy's head snapped towards his father. His closed eyes were partly covered by his messy brown hair. His mouth gaped open with laboured breaths, panting, and buckling. His hands trembled with pain. His head rotated, twisting like a hawk on the hunt, turning like an owl staring down a rat, towards the ankle. Tears streamed down his face, dripping onto the bed beneath him. Hair whipped his eyelids, his twisted face locked onto that God damned ankle.

Quiet as a whisper, he breathed out "T-They're coming. T-T-They are T-They're—" His head thrashed to the ceiling, "THE GYM IS COMING! JIMMM! THE GYM IS COMMINGGGG THEY'RE COMMMINNGGGGG! GYM! COMING! THE JIM IS COMMINGGG!!!" He paused. He held dad's leg above his head, gasping, and panting. "They are coming… No. No, they're coming!" his voice sobbed, subdued and broken, his shoulders shaking.

The boy's hands relaxed, and then tightened again. His body quivered. Stuttered breaths wracked through his small frame, sobs shook through his whole body, tears dripped onto the hardwood floor. Mom's ashen face, partly obscured by her hands, turned towards her husband. Eyes franticly searched each other, looking for an answer that didn't exist. Dad winced. His ankle ached as the pressure increased and decreased with no rhythm or pattern. The moment dragged on. The deathly grip of the boy's hand was unable to maintain the constant pressure. It spasmed, inconsistent and weaker, frailer as time went on. Mom got up from the bed. Her eyes cautious, but warm.

"William, are- what's wrong?" A hesitant hand came to the boy's shoulder, but the only response she got was his pleading voice.

"Gym C-Coming— T-They're coming. Jim. They're — they're coming. Gym." She touched his hand. The hand was, gently, pried off her husband's leg with no resistance. She moved an arm around her son's shoulder. He passively allowed her to lead him out of the room, his soft voice audible through it all. She got him to the door, and he walked past her through the dark hallway, into his room without her prompting. He lifted the covers and entered his bed and pulled his blankets back over himself.

"Gym… Gym… Jim… Jim…" his sobs whispered out into room as she stood at his bedroom door, hand clasped over her sobbing mouth, head nestled in her husband's arms.

William scribbled on paper, half listening to the story he'd heard dozens of times. He stood, marching towards the kitchen sink. Dad rambled on, the family's attention towards him. Really, everyone in the family knew the story. Each of them could tell it from memory alone. The stories were indistinguishable at this point, mingling and twisting and merging together. The stories started to coil into one another years ago, parts and excerpts shared and inserted amongst the different stories, but they listened anyway.

William watched his family. He watched their happy smiles, their laughs, their delight, their excitement. They hadn't joked and told stories like this for a while now. They were happiest when they were together, telling each other stories, enjoying each others company, talking for the sake of talking. They were happiest when they embraced their love and trust in one another, and shared their love and trust through their stories, through their joy, through their family. They were happiest when they gathered together simply because they wanted to, because they enjoyed talking to their family and telling each other stories.

The conversation was shifting to Ben's big one now, the biggest story they had. The story's realism was less and less relevant. Ben had told the story so many times, with so many versions, so many POV's, so many variants, that the original was insignificant. That story, the actual sleepwalking, the original story, was boring after all. It couldn't grip an audience, it had no flair, no hook, no style, no drama! Ben, while not quite the orator his dad was, could tell a good story, and story tellers liked to embellish their stories. All eyes and ears gave their attention to Ben: this was his favorite. After all, it was the first, and only, time his brother attacked him.

Ben was asleep. His snores were quiet, a quieter racket than his father's thunderous volume. It was a gentle murmur in his little room, the mumble of a young teenager. He didn't hear the activity in his brothers' room, the soft thumps that continued well past midnight, the rhythmic beating of hard against soft, the muffled strikes of young flesh against soft fabric. The sounds were unnoticed by everyone. If Ben was awake, he'd assume it was William messing around in his room, as he sometimes did. The young man wouldn't think anything of the sounds. Maybe, at most, he'd think it was odd that his brother was awake at such a late hour, but he wouldn't think beyond those initial musings. Regardless, Ben slept through the sounds, unsuspecting and ill-prepared for what was to come.

William stumbled into Ben's room. He held a sword in his hand. The plastic *Lord of the Rings* costume piece was clasped in his sweaty palm. The toy glinted in the soft red light from the bedside clock. Eyes, half open, stared unblinking at his brother's sleeping form. He staggered forward, colliding with his brother's school bag. The bag was stuffed with binders and books, the collision made them spew across the floor like Niagara Falls flowing into an inch-deep puddle. His feet crashed through the schoolbag's contents. Ben snored softly. William padded to the night-table, next to the young man's head. The open window, and the alarm clock's red glare, illuminated the boy's body. The sword gleamed in the red light, shining in the dark: a beacon of dread, a beacon of hatred, a beacon of violence, a corrupt sun. Above his head the sword loomed, steady and confident, the red glare flashing across the blade and his half-opened eyes. He waited. Minutes passed and his watery, teary, blurred eyes raked across the bed. The eyes sliced towards the still form of his brother. His tears dripped down onto the blue bed sheets. Blurry eyes focused on the sleeping body until it was all that remained, until it was all that mattered. The eyes swept across that soft warm flesh, the helpless, exposed, weak skin covered by a thin blue sheet. The quiet breathing, the low nasally snort that followed every so often, was peaceful, calm, relaxed, serene. The dark blue blankets covered his brother's body. The boy's sword glinted in the red light, reflecting stray beams into his teary eyes. He stared at his brother's pale skin, almost hidden by that dark blue blanket. His stare trailed to the pale hand that rested next to the covered, vulnerable face, to his black hair, to those black eyelashes, to his pale forehead, to his black hair covering those black eyes—

The black hair that covered the open black eyes, the bleary, confused blinking eyes that looked up at William, dazed.

"…Willia-?" The sword swept down, striking onto Ben's shoulder, hitting with a smack! "Ahh!" Ben jolted in his bed. His screams bounced off the walls. "Argh! William!" The sword flew towards his face, slashing into Ben's hastily raised arm. The old, weak plastic shattered, splintering down the middle. Fumbling in his tangled bedsheets, Ben looked through his bleeding fingers at his brother. William's body loomed over his, shadowed, hazy and indistinct, against the dark wall. The reddened, broken, foreboding sword was held aloft by his head. The fractured shards loosely clung to the sword. The soft plastic ridges tangled together, barely holding its shape. The shredded plastic blade was like a serrated steak knife and as long as a child's golf club. The red light encapsulated the sword and his brother's face. Tear marks streaked across his cheeks. The salty droplets splattered against the bedsheets. His brother's side was imbued by the faint, ethereal red light. Dozens of tears streamed down his cheeks, his red imbued eyes locked on his brother's panicked face. The sword, the arm, raised, ready to pounce, a warning of the future, a cat playing with its food, a tiger finding its prey, a lion slaying its own young. Ben franticly sat up, shouting "Ahh! Oww! Wil— What the Hell!? What are you doing?! William! Willia—! What!? Uhm, Whuh tuuh— William? -" The sword moved away. The red glare dissipated. The eyes returned to the darkness. The boy shuffled backward. His eyes locked on Ben. William's breath came in short intervals, gasping, wheezing, humming. His tear-streaked face punctured his brother's eyes. Shadowed in the darkness, his haunted, hallow, exhausted eyes shone with yet more unshed tears. Ben sat in his bed, watching quietly as his bag was righted, his books neatly packed into the bag. The shadow staggered out of his room, those eyes never left his face, the broken sword still held high. A breath sounded out. Ben wasn't aware he was holding it. Listening to William open his own door and climb back into his bed, Ben trembled. Ben stood, grasping his bleeding, bruised, and hurt arm. Wind whistled through the old house, only just audible over the old heater. He held his hands up to his head, shivering in the suddenly too hot winter air. He walked back towards his room, the bathroom first aid kit in his grasp. The lights showed the webbed streaks of cuts and bruises across his arm, the stains, and bits of plastic still on his bed. He placed the torn packaging into his trash bin, wrapping his arm and hand tightly. He crumpled onto the ground and leaned back against the wall

"Huh. God damnit, not again."

William stared at the ceiling. He lay in his bed. His hand balanced a plastic sword against the wall. He watched the sword, its blue plastic contrasted against the dark drywall. The sword tipped away, falling to the soft bed.

William stared at the blue plastic sword. That sword brought his family together, the silly costume piece brought his family happiness, joy, elation, companionship, kinship, love, friendship, affection. The sword was the catalyst, this time, for their entire day, it was the adhesive which kept them talking, kept them laughing, kept them happy, with each other. The sword gave them their conversation, their closeness, it held their bonds in its flimsy plastic frame and accepted their love for each other in its hollow form.

The sword didn't do anything itself. The sword couldn't do anything, it was a hunk of plastic, a glorified bit of landfill that would sit discarded and unused for centuries to come. The sword didn't do anything, yet it gave the family their happiness. William, his brother, his mother, his father, gave it influence over their emotions. The family projected their love onto the sword, and it accepted the burden, because it was just a plastic sword.

Sometimes, the stories they told each other weren't true, they all knew that, and they didn't care. They understood the sword was still intact, they understood William didn't cut his brothers arm, they understood he didn't scream at his father's foot, they understood that he didn't drool on himself, half naked in the dead of the Canadian winter, they understood that these were stories, fiction, words, and nothing more.

They didn't care about the actual event. They didn't care about the factually correct version of those fateful nights. The truth wasn't always a good story, so they didn't tell the true story.

They cared about their love for each other, they cared about their time together, their laughter and conversation together.

They cared about the truth when the truth was the point of the story. They told the truth when the truth was needed, was proper, was honourable, was helpful, was unhelpful, when it was brutal, when it was real, when it was honest, when it was necessary.

Rather, they cared about the truth when the truth was the story.

When the truth didn't matter, when they didn't care about reality, they told fanciful stories to their son, to their mother, to their father, to their brother.

They told fanciful stories to the people they loved and weren't concerned with whether they were true or not, whether they were authentic and representative of reality.

They told fanciful stories because they wanted to tell fanciful stories.

They told fanciful stories because they and their family liked to tell fanciful stories.

They told fanciful stories because they liked to hear fanciful stories.

They told fanciful stories because they loved and were loved.

William stared at the sword.

"And I think that's fine."

He placed the sword back into his closet.

Thank you for buying *Lukewarm Tea*, my first short story collection! I hope you enjoyed it. I have more stories coming, so please keep an eye out for my work as I finish them!

I'd like to thank my family, my mom, my dad, my brother, my cousins, my uncles, my aunts, and my grand parents, for supporting me through my life, through my writing. Thank you for helping me create this collection. I'd like to thank them for inspiring my creativity and letting me see those ideas through. Thank you.

I'd like to give a special thanks to my editor Tehjae Tsukada for giving such wonderful help in making this collection.

This is the first collection I'm publishing, and I hope you stick around to read my other stories.

ABOUT THE AUTHOR

William Foster was born in Brampton. He lives in Mississauga. He is a *University of Toronto Mississauga* alumni with an H.B.A. as an English Specialist. *Lukewarm Tea* is his first published short story collection.